Dragonfly Where Faith Takes Flight

A CHRISTIAN JOURNEY OF TRANSFORMATION AND TRIUMPH OVER ADVERSITY

Tammy Corwin

Words Matter Publishing
P.O. Box 1190
Decatur, Il 62525
www.wordsmatterpublishing.com

ISBN 13: 978-1-962467-35-3

Library of Congress Catalog Card Number: 2024942616

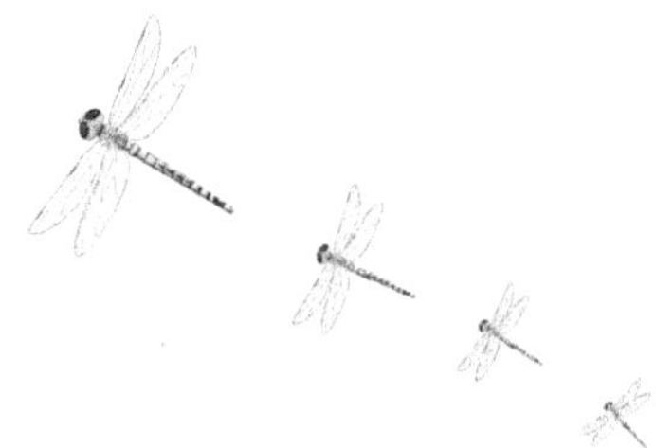

Preface

From a Biblical perspective, dragonflies are not mentioned directly in the scriptures. However, we can draw parallels and extract symbolism by aligning the characteristics and life cycle of dragonflies with broader Biblical themes such as creation, transformation, and spiritual insight.

1. Creation and Divine Design

Dragonflies, like all creatures, can be seen as a testament to God's creativity and attention to detail. Their intricate wing patterns, vibrant colors, and the precision of their flight reflect the complexity and beauty of God's creation.

Psalm 104:24 states: "How many are your works, LORD! In wisdom you made them all; the earth is full of your creatures." This can apply to the dragonfly's unique design and ecological role.

2. Metamorphosis and Transformation

The transformation from nymph to adult dragonfly, which involves significant changes in form and habitat, can be seen as a metaphor for spiritual renewal and transformation that is often discussed in the Bible.

2 Corinthians 5:17 says: "Therefore, if anyone is in Christ, the new creation has come: The old has gone, the new is here!" This verse parallels the metamorphosis of dragonflies, symbolizing the transformation of believers into new creations through faith in Christ.

3. Vision and Spiritual Insight

Dragonflies have exceptional 360-degree vision, allowing them to be aware of their surroundings at all times. This can be likened to the spiritual insight and discernment that believers are encouraged to develop.

Ephesians 1:18 prays that: "The eyes of your understanding being enlightened; that ye may know what is the hope of his calling, and what the riches of the glory of his inheritance in the saints," reflecting the idea that believers should seek spiritual clarity and awareness.

4. Symbols of Change and Resilience

The Dragonfly's ability to fly in all directions and adapt to new environments can symbolize the resilience and adaptability that Christians are called to embody. Despite challenges and changes, believers are encouraged to trust in God and navigate through life's changes with faith.

James 1:12 offers encouragement: "Blessed is the one who perseveres under trial because, having stood the test, that person will receive the crown of life that the Lord has promised to those who love him."

5. Indicator of Environmental and Spiritual Health

Just as dragonflies can indicate the health of an ecological environment, they can metaphorically remind Christians to evaluate their spiritual environments and their personal spiritual health.

Matthew 7:16-17 advises: "By their fruit you will recognize them. Do people pick grapes from thornbushes, or figs from thistles? Likewise, every good tree bears good fruit, but a bad tree bears bad fruit."

Conclusion

While dragonflies are not directly mentioned in the Bible, their life cycle and characteristics can provide Christians with symbolic lessons on transformation, divine creation, spiritual insight, and the importance of maintaining a healthy spiritual environment. These lessons encourage believers to seek continual growth and to be attentive to the workings of God in their lives.

Outline and Table of Contents

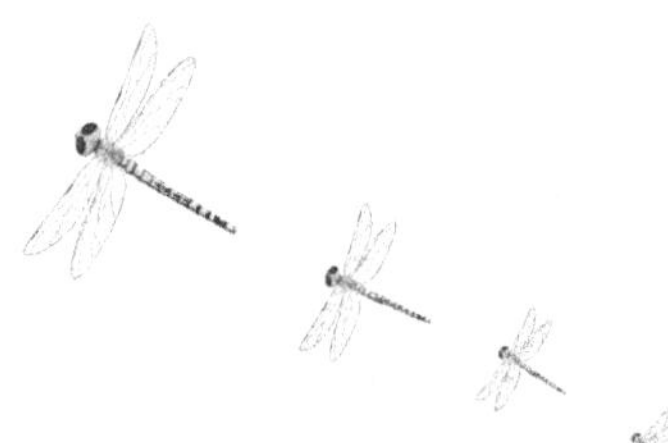

- Emphasis on becoming a new creation in Christ and living a life that reflects His teachings, inspired by Galatians 2:20: "I have been crucified with Christ and I no longer live, but Christ lives in me."
- Practical steps for aligning one's life more closely with Christian values.

- Strategies for living out one's faith consistently, supported by Philippians 1:6: "Being confident of this, that he who began a good work in you will carry it on to completion until the day of Christ Jesus."
- Importance of community, church, and continual spiritual disciplines like prayer and Bible study.

- Discussion on living a life of purpose and ongoing spiritual growth, inspired by the life of Christ and teachings such as those found in Matthew 5:16: "In the same way, let your light shine before others, that they may see your good deeds and glorify your Father in heaven."
- Encouragement to engage in lifelong learning, service, and evangelism.

- Summation of the journey of transformation encourages readers to continue walking in faith and growing in their relationship with God.
- Final reflections on spiritual growth as a continuous process that enriches one's personal life and community.

"Dragonfly Where Faith Takes Flight" will not only guide you through personal transformation but also deepen your faith, understanding, and commitment to living according to biblical principles.

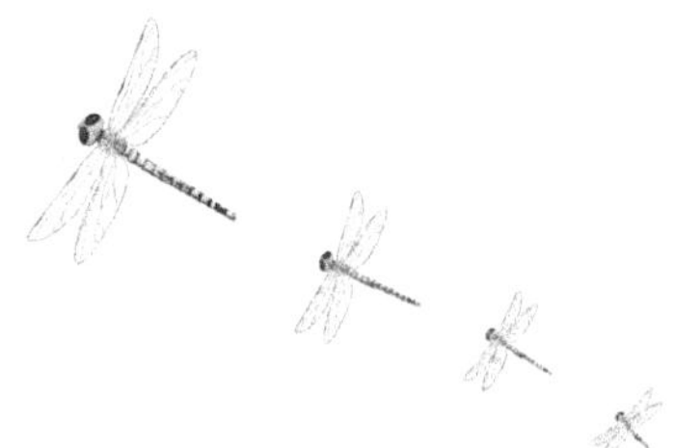

A Christian Journey of Transformation"

*W*elcome to "Dragonfly Where Faith Takes Flight," a guide designed to walk you through the profound process of personal and spiritual transformation from a Christian perspective. Just as the dragonfly undergoes a dramatic metamorphosis, emerging with new life and the ability to soar, we too are called to transform into new creations in Christ.

This book will take you through ten steps, each grounded in biblical wisdom and practical application, aimed at fostering growth and renewal in your life. Whether you're navigating challenges, seeking a deeper connection with God, or striving to align your life more closely with His Word, this journey is for you.

"Therefore, if anyone is in Christ, the new creation has come: The old has gone, the new is here!" (2 Corinthians 5:17). This verse captures the essence of our journey—a transformation so profound that it touches every aspect of our being, renewing our minds and hearts in the image of our Creator.

As we embark on this path, we'll explore not only the steps necessary for change but also the Christian virtues of faith, hope, love, forgiveness, and resilience. By integrating these into our lives, we are not merely changing; we are being transformed by the renewing of our minds, setting our sights on things above.

Let us begin this journey with open hearts and minds, ready to be transformed and to live out our faith in new and dynamic ways.

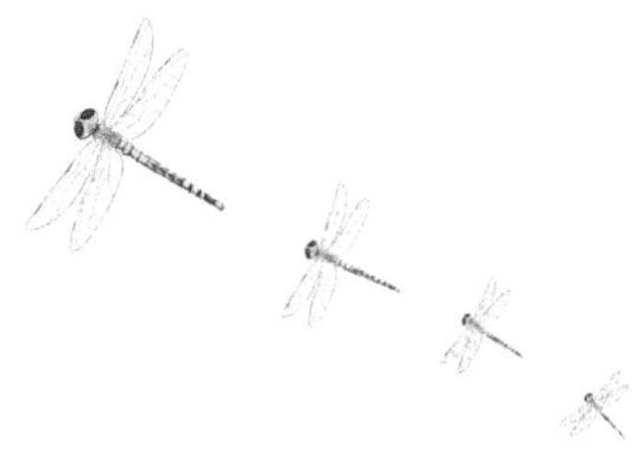

Chapter 1

Understanding Your Current State

Recognizing and Accepting Your Spiritual Condition

The first step in our transformation journey is to recognize and accept our current spiritual condition. This involves an honest self-assessment of our faith, behaviors, and life direction in relation to God's will.

Self-Assessment Through Scripture

King David, a man after God's own heart, understood the importance of self-examination. He invites God to search his heart through prayer, a practice we too can adopt:

"Search me, God, and know my heart; test me and know my anxious thoughts. See if there is any offensive way in me, and lead me in the way everlasting." (Psalm 139:23-24)

To start, take a quiet moment to pray this Scripture. Ask God to reveal areas in your life that need change or renewal. Reflect on aspects such as your prayer life, Bible study habits, community involvement, and personal conduct.

1

Acceptance: Embracing Your Reality

Accepting your current state doesn't mean complacency. Instead, it signifies recognizing where you stand as a starting point for growth. Jesus Christ offers us grace to accept ourselves and our imperfections, knowing that He is the potter and we are the clay (Isaiah 64:8).

Steps to Acceptance

1. **Identify Areas for Growth**: Make a list of spiritual and personal areas where you feel you need to grow. This might include increasing faith, controlling temper, or being more compassionate.

2. **Prayer for Acceptance and Guidance**: Engage in daily prayer, asking God to help you accept your current state and to provide guidance for the road ahead.

3. **Seek Wise Counsel**: Proverbs 15:22 tells us that plans fail for lack of counsel, but with many advisers, they succeed. Discuss your thoughts and feelings with a trusted pastor, mentor, or Christian friend who can offer biblical advice and encouragement.

Embracing Your Journey with Hope

As we acknowledge our starting point, we do so with hope. Romans 5:3-5 reminds us that suffering produces perseverance, perseverance character, and character hope. And hope does not put us to shame, because God's love has been poured out into our hearts through the Holy Spirit, who has been given to us.

Let this first step of understanding and accepting your current state be grounded in hope—a hope that does not disappoint because it is anchored in the love and promises of God.

As we conclude Chapter 1, remember that this is just the beginning. Each step on this path is designed to draw you closer to God and deeper into His transformative work in your life. In the next chapter, we will explore the biblical and practical aspects of embracing change, setting the stage for the renewing transformations that lie ahead.

Notes

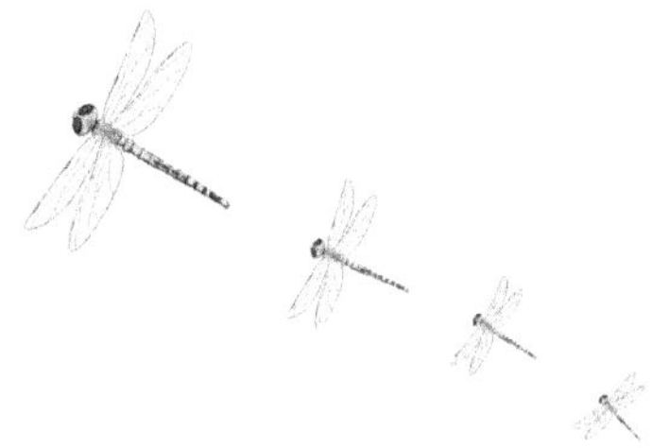

Chapter 2

Embracing Change

Welcoming God's Transformative Work

Change is a constant in the Christian life, reflecting our ongoing growth towards spiritual maturity. This chapter explores the biblical foundation for embracing change, offering practical insights on how to navigate transitions with faith and courage.

Biblical Foundations for Change

Change is often depicted in Scripture as an essential part of God's plan for His people. Romans 12:2 underscores this, urging us to not conform to this world, but be transformed by the renewing of our minds, so that we may discern what is the good, pleasing, and perfect will of God.

Abraham's Journey: Consider Abraham, who was called by God to leave everything familiar behind and step into the unknown (Genesis 12:1). His willingness to embrace God's changes led to the birth of a nation.

Understanding the Nature of Change

Change can be unsettling because it challenges our sense of security and familiarity. However, it is also an opportunity for growth and deepening our reliance on God.

1. **Spiritual Growth**: Just as seasons change, our spiritual lives also go through seasons of growth, pruning, and harvesting (John 15:1-2).

2. **Character Development**: God often uses change to refine our character, as seen in the trials of Joseph, which prepared him for leadership and reconciliation (Genesis 50:20).

Embracing Uncertainty with Faith

Facing the unknown requires faith—a trust in God's goodness and His overarching plans for our lives.

Scriptural Encouragement: Hebrews 11:1 defines faith as confidence in what we hope for and assurance about what we do not see. This is the faith that enabled the heroes of the Bible to embrace their divinely ordained changes.

Steps to Embrace Change

To actively engage with and embrace the changes God brings into your life, consider these practical steps grounded in scriptural truths:

1. **Pray for Openness**: Ask God to help you be open to the changes He is bringing into your life. Prayer aligns our hearts with God's will, as Jesus modeled in Gethsemane (Matthew 26:39).

2. **Study Biblical Examples of Change**: Regularly reading and meditating on Bible stories that involve significant changes can provide inspiration and courage. Stories like those of Ruth, Esther, and Paul show how God masterfully works through changes in our lives.

3. **Community Support**: Share your experiences and feelings about change with your church community. Galatians 6:2 encourages us to bear one another's burdens, and in doing so, fulfill the law of Christ.

4. **Reflect on Past Changes**: Reflecting on how you've seen God work through previous changes in your life can bolster your faith. Create a "faith journal" where you document these instances and the outcomes.

Cultivating a Heart for Change

Developing a heart that is receptive to change involves cultivating qualities like flexibility, humility, and a readiness to step out in faith.

- **Flexibility**: Be willing to adjust your plans and ideas in response to God's leading.

- **Humility**: Recognize that God's ways and thoughts are higher than ours (Isaiah 55:9).

- **Courage**: Step out in faith even when the path isn't fully clear, trusting that God's grace is sufficient for you (2 Corinthians 12:9).

Conclusion

Embracing change is not merely about adjusting to new circumstances; it's about embracing God's transformative work in your life. It requires faith, courage, and a commitment to follow wherever He leads. As you open your heart to the changes God brings, you are stepping into the fullness of life He has prepared for you. In the next chapter, we will explore how to set concrete goals within this framework of divine guidance and support.

Notes

Chapter 3

Setting Concrete Goals

Aligning Your Aspirations with God's Will

Goal-setting is a vital aspect of Christian life, helping us to focus our efforts in service to God and grow in accordance with His plans. In this chapter, we explore how to set goals that not only reflect our personal ambitions but are also deeply rooted in the values and teachings of Scripture.

The Biblical Basis for Goal-Setting

Scripture encourages us to live purposefully and intentionally, using the talents and resources God has given us to achieve His purposes. Consider the parable of the talents (Matthew 25:14-30), where the servants are entrusted with resources and expected to use them wisely. This parable teaches us about God's expectation for us to actively engage and multiply what we have been given, a principle that directly applies to setting and pursuing goals.

Principles of Christian Goal-Setting

When setting goals as a Christian, it's important to align them with God's word and His commandments. Our goals should not only aim for personal or professional growth but should also enhance our spiritual well-being and help us to serve others.

1. **God-Centered Goals**: Start with prayer, asking God to reveal His plans for you. As Proverbs 16:3 advises, "Commit to the LORD whatever you do, and he will establish your plans."

2. **S.M.A.R.T Goals**: Adapt the well-known S.M.A.R.T (Specific, Measurable, Achievable, Relevant, Time-bound) goals framework to ensure your goals are clear and reachable, but with a focus on spiritual alignment.

3. **Eternal Perspective**: Set goals that have eternal value. Consider how your goals help you grow in faith, serve others, and spread the Gospel. Matthew 6:20 reminds us, "But store up for yourselves treasures in heaven, where moths and vermin do not destroy, and where thieves do not break in and steal."

Setting and Pursuing Spiritual Goals

Setting spiritual goals can be a transformative practice that deepens your relationship with God and enhances your Christian walk.

1. **Daily Devotion**: Aim to spend dedicated time in prayer and Bible study each day. Setting a goal to read through the Bible in a year, or to study a particular book of the Bible in-depth, can provide spiritual nourishment and deeper understanding.

2. **Service**: Set goals related to serving within your church or community. This could involve volunteering for specific ministries or initiating outreach programs that reflect Christ's love to others.

3. **Character Development**: Identify aspects of the Fruit of the Spirit (Galatians 5:22-23) you wish to cultivate. Setting goals to grow in love, patience, kindness, or self-control can have profound impacts on your interactions and spiritual life.

Overcoming Obstacles in Goal Achievement

While pursuing our goals, we often encounter obstacles that require us to rely on God's strength and guidance.

- **Prayer and Fasting**: Utilize these spiritual disciplines to seek God's help and direction when challenges arise.

- **Accountability**: Share your goals with a trusted Christian friend or mentor who can provide support and accountability. Ecclesiastes 4:9 reminds us, "Two are better than one, because they have a good return for their labor."

Celebrating Achievements and Learning from Setbacks

Recognize and celebrate each achievement as a gift from God, giving thanks for His guidance and provision. Similarly, when facing setbacks, reflect on what God may be teaching you through the experience. James 1:2-4 encourages us to consider it pure joy when we face trials because these tests produce perseverance and maturity.

Conclusion

Setting concrete goals as a Christian means aligning your plans with God's will, seeking His guidance throughout the process, and aiming for outcomes that glorify Him. By doing so, you not only achieve personal and spiritual growth but also contribute to the Kingdom of God in meaningful ways. As you move forward, keep your heart and mind open to God's direction and be ready to adjust your plans according to His leading. In the next chapter, we will explore how to cultivate resilience, a critical attribute for navigating the journey of achieving these goals.

Notes

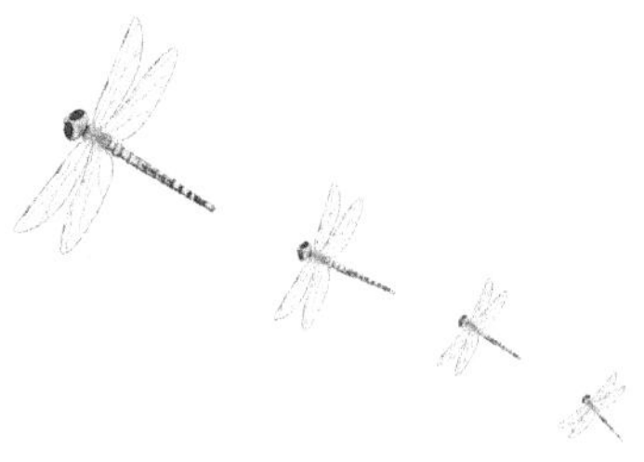

Chapter 4

Cultivating Resilience

Strengthening Your Faith Through Trials

Resilience in the Christian life is about more than enduring; it's about growing stronger through the trials we face, rooted in faith and trust in God. This chapter explores how to develop spiritual resilience, enabling you to withstand life's storms while maintaining a firm faith and a hopeful outlook.

Biblical Foundations of Resilience

The Bible is filled with stories of resilience. Consider Job, who, despite tremendous suffering and loss, declared, "Though he slay me, yet will I hope in him" (Job 13:15). Paul's letters from prison also demonstrate resilience, as he continued to preach the gospel and encourage others despite his circumstances (Philippians 1:12-14).

Understanding Spiritual Resilience

Spiritual resilience is the ability to sustain your faith and grow spiritually in the face of challenges and adversities. It involves:

25

1. **Deep Trust in God**: Believing that God is in control and has a purpose for your trials, as Romans 8:28 teaches, "And we know that in all things God works for the good of those who love him, who have been called according to his purpose."

2. **Hope**: Maintaining a forward-looking perspective, grounded in the promise of eternal life and the return of Jesus Christ.

Developing Resilience Through Spiritual Practices

Building resilience requires intentional practice and commitment to spiritual disciplines that strengthen your faith.

1. **Regular Bible Study and Meditation**: Immersing yourself in God's Word provides comfort and guidance, reinforcing your trust in God's promises. Psalm 119:50 says, "My comfort in my suffering is this: Your promise preserves my life."

2. **Persistent Prayer**: Communicating with God through prayer helps to fortify your spirit, offering peace and perseverance. Ephesians 6:18 urges us to "pray in the Spirit on all occasions with all kinds of prayers and requests."

3. **Fellowship with Believers**: Engaging with a community of faith provides support and encouragement. Hebrews 10:24-25 highlights the importance of meeting together to spur one another on toward love and good deeds.

Embracing Trials as Opportunities for Growth

Viewing challenges as opportunities to demonstrate and deepen your faith can transform your approach to hardship.

1. **Accept Trials as Spiritual Training**: James 1:2-4 encourages believers to consider trials as joy because they test faith, develop perseverance, and lead to maturity.

2. **Identify Lessons and Blessings**: In every difficulty, look for what God might be teaching you or how He is blessing you in other ways.

Applying Resilience in Daily Life

Integrating resilience into your daily life involves practical steps that make faith a living, breathing part of every day.

1. **Setbacks as Stepping Stones**: Use setbacks as opportunities to practice resilience by actively trusting in God's plan and recalibrating your approach based on His guidance.

2. **Service and Outreach**: Serving others can shift your focus from your struggles to the needs of others, providing perspective and a sense of purpose.

Maintaining Resilience Over Time

To sustain resilience, it's important to:

1. **Celebrate Milestones**: Acknowledge and celebrate moments when your resilience has led to spiritual breakthroughs or personal growth.

2. **Continue Learning and Growing**: Stay engaged with new biblical teachings, Christian literature, and teachings that can deepen your understanding and strengthen your faith.

Conclusion

Cultivating resilience is a key component of the Christian walk. It allows you to navigate life's challenges with grace and fortitude, always relying on the strength that God provides. By embracing and developing resilience, you prepare yourself not only to survive life's challenges but to thrive and witness for Christ through them.

In the next chapter, we will explore the transformative power of forgiveness, which both requires and reinforces spiritual resilience.

Notes

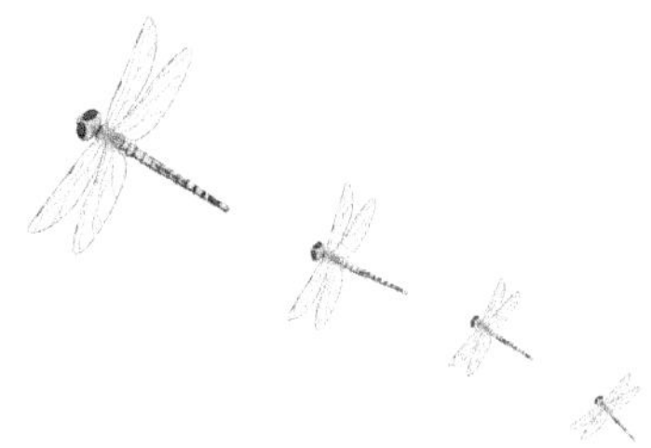

Chapter 5

Practicing Forgiveness

Embracing Freedom Through Forgiveness

Forgiveness is a central theme in Christianity, fundamental to the teachings of Jesus Christ. It is both a command and a gift, offering freedom from the burdens of bitterness and resentment. In this chapter, we will explore the spiritual significance of forgiveness, how it enhances resilience, and practical steps to forgive as Christ forgave us.

The Biblical Imperative to Forgive

The Scripture is replete with calls to forgive. In Ephesians 4:31-32, Paul instructs, "Let all bitterness and wrath and anger and clamor and slander be put away from you, along with all malice. Be kind to one another, tenderhearted, forgiving one another, as God in Christ forgave you." This passage not only commands forgiveness but also ties it directly to the example of Christ's infinite forgiveness.

Understanding Forgiveness

Forgiveness in the Christian context involves letting go of anger and resentment towards someone who has wronged you, choosing instead to extend mercy, despite your right to retaliate.

1. **Forgiveness is Not Forgetting**: Forgiving someone does not mean forgetting the wrong done. It means choosing to set aside vengeance and bitterness, trusting God to handle justice according to His perfect wisdom and timing.

2. **Forgiveness is a Process**: Sometimes, forgiveness requires a continual effort, especially for deep wounds. It might need to be chosen daily until the emotional healing catches up with the decision to forgive.

Steps to Practicing Forgiveness

Forgiving others can be challenging, particularly when the hurt is deep. However, the following biblical principles can guide you through the process:

1. **Reflect on God's Forgiveness**: Contemplate the vastness of God's forgiveness towards you. Romans 5:8 shows us that "God demonstrates His own love for us in this: While we were still sinners, Christ died for us." Remembering this can inspire us to extend forgiveness to others.

2. **Pray for a Forgiving Heart**: Ask God to soften your heart and give you the strength to forgive. Matthew 5:44 advises, "But I tell you, love your enemies and pray for those who persecute you."

3. **Let Go of the Right to Get Even**: Embrace Romans 12:19, where Paul writes, "Do not take revenge, my dear friends, but leave room for God's wrath, for it is written: 'It is mine to avenge; I will repay,' says the Lord."

4. **Seek Reconciliation When Possible**: While forgiveness can be given regardless of the offender's response, reconciliation requires the cooperation of both parties. Pursue peace as far as it depends on you (Romans 12:18).

The Healing Power of Forgiveness

Forgiveness can lead to profound spiritual and emotional healing. Here are some of the ways it can transform your life:

1. **Freedom from Anger and Resentment**: Forgiveness liberates you from the toxic cycle of anger, allowing you to experience peace and joy.

2. **Improved Relationships**: Forgiving and seeking forgiveness can heal and strengthen relationships, creating deeper bonds of trust and love.

3. **Spiritual Growth**: Forgiving others deepens your understanding of God's grace and draws you closer to Him.

Living Out Forgiveness

To truly live a life of forgiveness, consider these daily practices:

1. **Daily Self-Examination**: At the end of each day, reflect on any feelings of bitterness that may have arisen and choose to forgive anew.

2. **Community Support**: Share your struggles and victories with trusted Christian friends who can provide support and accountability.

3. **Embrace Grace**: Continuously remind yourself of the grace you have received in Christ, and let that grace overflow to others in your life.

Conclusion

Forgiveness is not just an occasional act, but a crucial part of the Christian lifestyle, essential for personal peace and spiritual vitality. By learning to forgive as God forgives, you not only obey Christ's teachings but also mirror His merciful character to the world, promoting healing and reconciliation.

In the next chapter, we will explore the journey of overcoming trauma, another critical aspect of spiritual and emotional healing and resilience.

Notes

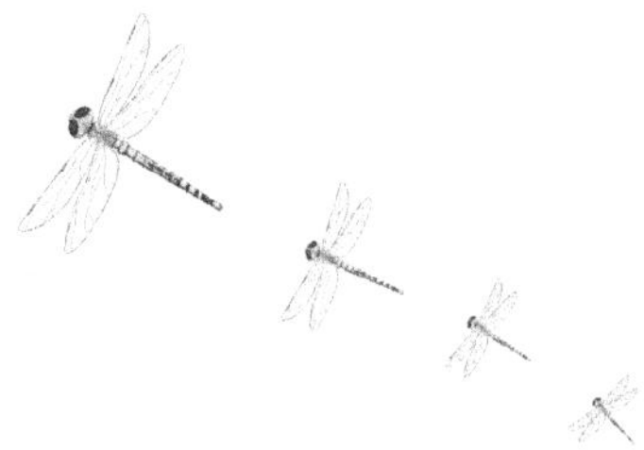

Chapter 6

Overcoming Trauma

Healing Through Christ

Trauma can deeply affect one's life, creating long-lasting emotional and psychological wounds. In the Christian journey, overcoming trauma involves turning towards Christ for healing and using one's faith to find strength and renewal. This chapter explores the scriptural approach to healing from trauma and offers practical steps grounded in Christian principles.

Understanding Trauma from a Christian Perspective

Trauma disrupts our sense of security and can often make us question God's goodness or His presence in our lives. However, the Bible offers many promises of God's constant support and healing, showing us that He is near to the brokenhearted and saves the crushed in spirit (Psalm 34:18).

Biblical Figures Who Overcame Trauma

Many biblical figures experienced significant trauma yet found healing through their faith:

- **Job**: After immense suffering and loss, Job's story is a powerful testament to enduring faith in God's sovereignty and goodness, despite not understanding His ways.

- **Joseph**: Betrayed by his brothers and unjustly imprisoned, Joseph eventually saw God's purpose in his sufferings—to preserve many lives (Genesis 50:20).

Steps to Healing from Trauma

The journey to healing from trauma can be complex and requires both time and active participation in the healing process, underpinned by faith in God.

1. **Seek God's Comfort in Prayer and Scripture**: Regularly engage in prayer, asking God to heal your wounds and restore your spirit. Meditate on scriptures that affirm God's nearness and care, such as Isaiah 43:2, which promises that when you pass through the waters, God will be with you.

2. **Participate in Christian Counseling**: Seek out counselors who integrate biblical truths with psychological expertise. This approach can provide both spiritual and clinical support, addressing the emotional and psychological aspects of trauma.

3. **Build a Supportive Community**: Connect with a church community that understands and supports people experiencing trauma. Fellowship with others who have had similar experiences can provide encouragement and decrease feelings of isolation.

4. **Forgiveness**: While incredibly challenging, forgiveness can be a powerful step towards healing. Forgiving those who have caused trauma does not diminish the wrong done but can liberate you from the cycle of anger and hurt.

5. **Engage in Service**: Serving others can shift focus from self to service, providing purpose and joy. Helping others who are suffering can also bring perspective and healing to your own wounds.

Healing as a Process

Recognize that healing from trauma is a process, not a one-time event. It involves:

- **Patience with Yourself**: Allow yourself the time to grieve and heal, understanding that healing cannot be rushed.

- **Continual Prayer and Trust in God**: Maintain an ongoing dialogue with God, expressing your fears, frustrations, and hopes.

- **Regular Reflection**: Keep a journal of your healing journey, noting moments of difficulty as well as breakthroughs, which can serve as reminders of God's faithfulness.

Testimonies of Healing

Encourage healing through sharing and listening to testimonies within your community. Hearing how God has worked in the lives of others can bolster your faith and inspire patience and perseverance in your healing journey.

Conclusion

Overcoming trauma through Christ involves anchoring your hope in God's unchanging character and promises. It requires the support of a compassionate community and a commitment to the healing process. As you continue to seek God's healing and practice these biblical principles, remember that He is making all things new, including your heart and life (Revelation 21:5).

In the next chapter, we will explore managing loss and grief, continuing our journey through healing and spiritual growth.

Notes

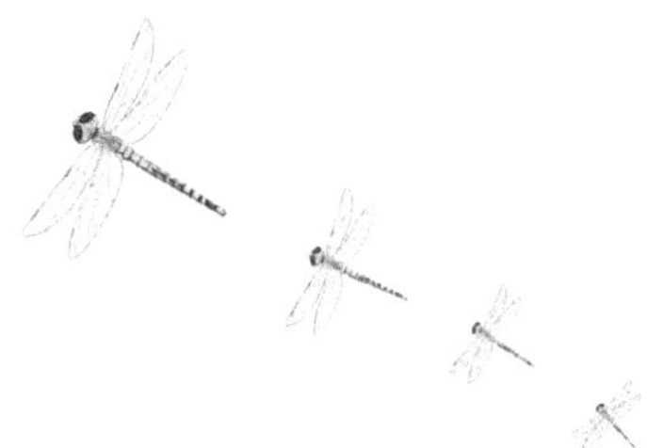

Chapter 7

Managing Loss and Grief

Finding Comfort and Hope in Christ

Loss and grief are profound human experiences that touch every life at some point. For Christians, managing these experiences is deeply intertwined with faith, drawing on God's promises of comfort, resurrection, and eternal life. This chapter explores how to navigate the difficult waters of loss and grief through a Christian lens, offering scriptural support and practical guidance.

Biblical Insights into Loss and Grief

The Bible does not shy away from the reality of grief and loss but addresses it with profound empathy and hope. Jesus Himself expressed deep sorrow at the tomb of His friend Lazarus, demonstrating that mourning is a natural and human response to loss (John 11:35).

- **David's Lament**: King David expressed his grief openly through lamentation and poetry, as seen in 2 Samuel 1:17-27, providing a model for using creative expression as a cathartic outlet.

The Role of Faith in Grieving

Faith does not eliminate the pain of loss, but it provides a framework for understanding and processing grief.

1. **Hope in Resurrection**: Christians grieve with the hope of the resurrection, knowing that death is not the end. As Paul writes in 1 Thessalonians 4:13-14, we do not grieve as those who have no hope, for we believe that Jesus died and rose again.

2. **God's Comfort**: The Scriptures offer numerous promises of God's comfort to the grieving, such as Psalm 34:18, which assures that the Lord is close to the brokenhearted and saves those who are crushed in spirit.

Practical Steps for Managing Grief

While each person's journey through grief is unique, certain practices can help manage the emotional and spiritual challenges of grieving.

1. **Lean on Your Church Community**: Engage with your church family for support. The fellowship and understanding they offer can be a powerful source of comfort and strength.

2. **Prayer and Meditation**: Maintain an active prayer life and meditate on God's Word. This spiritual discipline helps anchor your heart and mind in the truths of God's sovereignty and love.

3. **Memorialize the Lost**: Creating ways to remember loved ones can aid the grieving process. This could include establishing a scholarship, planting a garden, or other acts that honor their memory and reflect their values.

4. **Professional Christian Counseling**: Sometimes, the weight of grief might require the support of a professional. Christian counselors or therapists trained in grief counseling can provide valuable guidance and support.

5. **Journaling**: Writing down your thoughts and feelings can be a therapeutic way to process grief. Reflecting on scriptural promises as you journal can also bring spiritual comfort and insight.

Embracing Healing in Christ

Healing from grief is a gradual process that involves embracing the pain and moving through it with the help of the Holy Spirit.

- **Allow Yourself to Grieve**: Give yourself permission to experience all the emotions that come with grief without judgment. Ecclesiastes 3:4 reminds us there is "a time to weep and a time to laugh, a time to mourn and a time to dance."

- **Seek Renewed Purpose**: In time, seeking a renewed sense of purpose can help mitigate the pain of loss. Engage in activities that are meaningful to you and that can benefit others, turning your grief into a catalyst for new growth.

Conclusion

While loss and grief are inevitable aspects of the human experience, they do not have to overwhelm us. Through Christ, we can find the strength to endure, the comfort to soothe our pain, and the hope to look forward with confidence to a future where God will wipe away every tear from our eyes (Revelation 21:4). In the next chapter, we will discuss the transformative power of reinventing oneself through Christ, building on the changes and growth experienced through overcoming grief and trauma.

Notes

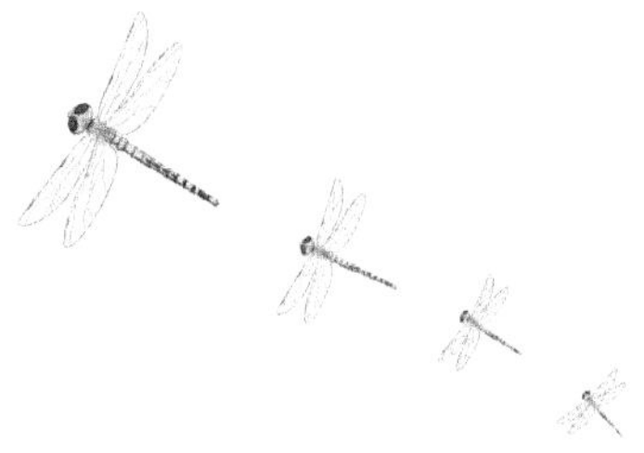

Chapter 8

Reinventing Yourself

A Christian Approach to Personal Transformation

Reinvention, in the Christian context, is not merely about changing aspects of your life for personal or professional gain but is deeply rooted in spiritual renewal and aligning more closely with God's purposes. This chapter explores how Christians can approach reinventing themselves to reflect Christ more fully in their lives and actions.

Biblical Basis for Reinvention

The concept of personal transformation is foundational in Scripture, where it is often depicted as a spiritual rebirth or renewal. Paul describes this transformation in 2 Corinthians 5:17: "Therefore, if anyone is in Christ, the new creation has come: The old has gone, the new is here!" This passage highlights the profound, holistic change that occurs when we live through Christ.

Understanding Christian Reinvention

Reinvention in the Christian life involves examining our lives under the guidance of the Holy Spirit and making conscious decisions to align more closely with the teachings of Christ. This process includes:

1. **Spiritual Renewal**: Continuously seeking to grow in faith and deepen your relationship with God.

2. **Behavioral Change**: Modifying behaviors and habits to better reflect Christian values.

3. **Vocational and Relational Adjustments**: Aligning your career and relationships with your spiritual convictions.

Steps to Reinventing Yourself

Reinvention is an active process that requires prayerful consideration and practical steps. Here's how you can begin:

1. **Pray for Divine Guidance**: Start with prayer, asking God to reveal areas of your life that need change and to empower you with the Holy Spirit to make these changes.

2. **Study the Word**: Immerse yourself in Scripture, letting God's Word shape your thoughts, attitudes, and actions. Romans 12:2 underscores this, urging us not to conform to the pattern of this world but be transformed by the renewing of our minds.

3. **Seek Accountability**: Share your desire for change with a trusted spiritual mentor or a small group in your church. Accountability can provide support and encouragement as you make changes.

4. **Implement Gradual Changes**: Focus on one area of your life at a time. Whether it's improving your prayer life, being more patient and loving in your relationships, or making career choices that reflect your Christian values, small, consistent changes lead to substantial transformation over time.

Living Out the New You

As you make these changes, it's essential to actively live out your new identity in Christ in everyday situations:

1. **Service**: Look for opportunities to serve within your church and community, which can reinforce your new identity and purpose.

2. **Witnessing**: Share your faith and how God is working in your life with others. This not only strengthens your own faith but can also encourage and draw others to Christ.

3. **Continuous Learning**: Keep learning and growing in your faith through Bible studies, Christian books, seminars, and teachings.

Overcoming Challenges in Reinvention

Change is often met with internal and external resistance. Overcoming these challenges requires perseverance and reliance on God:

1. **Expect Resistance**: Be prepared for spiritual warfare. Arm yourself with the whole armor of God (Ephesians 6:10-18) to stand against the challenges.

2. **Embrace Grace**: When you falter, remember that God's grace is sufficient for you. His power is made perfect in weakness (2 Corinthians 12:9).

Conclusion

Reinventing yourself as a Christian means embracing a life that gloriously reflects Christ in all aspects. It's about becoming a new creation, equipped and inspired to do good works, which God prepared in advance for us to do (Ephesians 2:10). As we continue to grow and transform, we move closer to the person God has designed us to be, bringing glory to Him and His kingdom.

In the next chapter, we will explore how to maintain this new self and ensure that the changes have a lasting impact on your life and the lives of those around you.

Notes

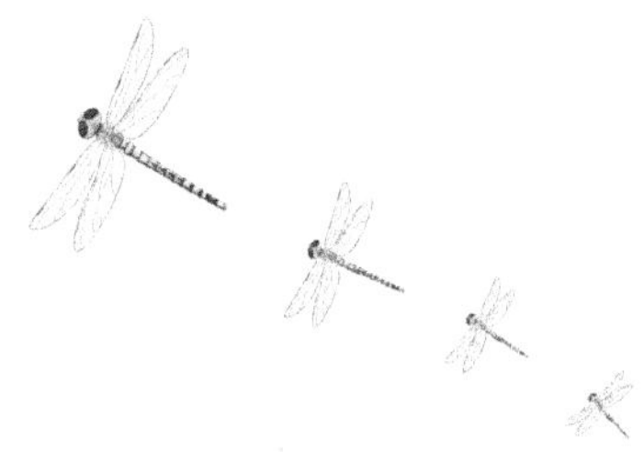

Chapter 9

Maintaining Your New Self

Sustaining Transformation in Christ

After embarking on a journey of personal and spiritual reinvention, the next crucial phase is maintaining these changes. This chapter focuses on how to sustain the transformation you've achieved through continuous reliance on God, ongoing spiritual practices, and active participation in the Christian community.

The Importance of Ongoing Spiritual Discipline

Maintaining your new self in Christ is not a passive experience but requires active engagement with spiritual disciplines that nurture and strengthen your faith.

1. **Consistent Prayer Life**: Continue to cultivate a deep prayer life, which is essential for staying connected to God and seeking His guidance daily.

2. **Regular Bible Study**: Make Scripture reading and study a daily habit. The Word of God is living and active (Hebrews 4:12) and provides wisdom, encouragement, and correction needed to sustain your transformation.

3. **Fellowship with Believers**: Regular participation in church life and small groups helps keep you accountable and supported in your walk with Christ.

Techniques for Sustaining Change

The journey of maintaining your new self can be supported by several practical approaches that encourage growth and prevent backsliding.

1. **Setting Ongoing Goals**: Continue to set spiritual and personal goals that challenge you to grow in your faith and apply it in all areas of life.

2. **Seeking Accountability**: Maintain relationships with mentors and peers who encourage your growth and hold you accountable. As Proverbs 27:17 says, "As iron sharpens iron, so one person sharpens another."

3. **Embracing Service**: Regular involvement in service projects and ministry opportunities can reinforce your new identity in Christ and provide practical ways to live out your faith.

Responding to Life's Challenges

Challenges and setbacks are inevitable, but they can be faced effectively with the right spiritual tools and mindset.

1. **Rely on God's Strength**: Recognize that your ability to maintain change does not rely solely on your strength but on God's power working through you (Philippians 4:13).

2. **Adaptive Growth**: Be open to the Holy Spirit's leading, even if it means further changes or adjustments in your life. Stay flexible and teachable, understanding that spiritual growth is a lifelong process.

3. **Resilience Through Trials**: Use trials as opportunities to practice resilience and deepen your trust in God. James 1:2-4 encourages believers to consider trials as joy because they produce perseverance, leading to maturity.

Celebrating Milestones

As you continue in your transformed life, it's important to celebrate milestones and reflect on the progress you've made.

1. **Spiritual Milestones**: Celebrate anniversaries of significant spiritual decisions or achievements, such as baptism anniversaries or years of ministry service.

2. **Reflective Practices**: Regularly take time to reflect on how you have grown and changed. Keeping a spiritual journal can be a helpful tool for this practice.

Conclusion

Maintaining your new self in Christ is a dynamic and continuous journey that involves much more than simply avoiding old habits. It's about living a life fully devoted to Christ, growing in grace, and being transformed day by day into His likeness. As you implement these practices, remember that you are not alone—God is with you, His Spirit empowers you, and His people support you.

In the next chapter, we will conclude by exploring how to live fully as a transformed individual, continuing to grow in faith and impact the world around you.

Notes

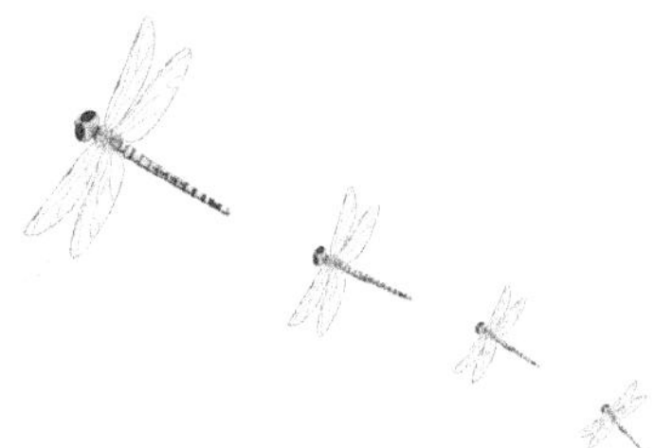

Chapter 10

Living as a Dragonfly

Embodying Continuous Spiritual Growth

*L*iving as a dragonfly in the Christian context means embodying continuous spiritual growth, actively engaging in God's kingdom, and maintaining a lifestyle that reflects the transformation you have undergone. This final chapter offers insights on how to live fully in your new identity, influencing the world around you positively and persistently pursuing deeper communion with God.

Embracing a Life of Continuous Transformation

Living transformed is not a static state but a continuous journey of becoming more like Christ. This requires constant attention to your spiritual life and an openness to ongoing change.

1. **Lifelong Learning**: Commit to being a lifelong learner of Scripture and the Christian faith. Engage regularly with biblical teachings, theological insights, and spiritual writings that challenge and deepen your understanding of God.

2. **Spiritual Maturity**: Focus on developing the fruits of the Spirit (Galatians 5:22-23), which signify mature Christian character. Evaluate your growth in love, joy, peace, patience, kindness, goodness, faithfulness, gentleness, and self-control.

3. **Ongoing Sanctification**: Sanctification is the process by which God makes us holy through His Spirit. Embrace this process by being open to conviction and correction from God's Word and His Spirit.

Applying Your Transformation in Daily Life

Transformed living should permeate every aspect of your life, influencing your actions, decisions, and interactions with others.

1. **Work and Vocation**: Dedicate your professional life to glorifying God, whether through excellence in your field, integrity in your dealings, or kindness to your colleagues.

2. **Relationships**: Let your relationships reflect Christ's love. This includes forgiveness, selflessness, and a commitment to building others up in faith and love.

3. **Community Engagement**: Actively participate in your community with the intent to serve and evangelize. Look for opportunities to volunteer, support local charities, and share the gospel.

Staying Rooted in Christ

The key to sustained transformation is staying deeply rooted in Christ. This involves several foundational practices:

1. **Regular Worship and Communion**: Prioritize regular worship and participation in the sacraments. These practices are vital for staying connected to Christ and the body of believers.

2. **Prayer and Fasting**: Maintain a disciplined practice of prayer and fasting. These spiritual disciplines draw you closer to God and strengthen your spirit for the challenges of daily life.

3. **Scriptural Meditation**: Make meditating on Scripture a daily habit. Use God's Word as the lens through which you view the world and make decisions.

Facing Challenges with Resilience

As you live out your transformation, you will inevitably face challenges and opposition. Equip yourself with biblical truths and the armor of God (Ephesians 6:10-18) to stand firm in your faith.

1. **Expect Trials**: Understand that trials are part of the Christian life and are used by God for your growth and His glory (James 1:2-4).

2. **Community Support**: Lean on your church community for support during tough times. The encouragement and prayers of fellow believers can be a lifeline.

Conclusion

Living as a dragonfly means embracing the beauty and freedom of your transformation in Christ and continuously growing in grace and truth. It involves spreading your wings in faith, soaring above life's challenges, and reflecting God's love in all you do. As you move forward, remember that your journey is a testament to God's power and grace, inspiring others to seek Him and embrace their own transformations. Keep flying high, knowing that you are being renewed day by day (2 Corinthians 4:16).

Notes

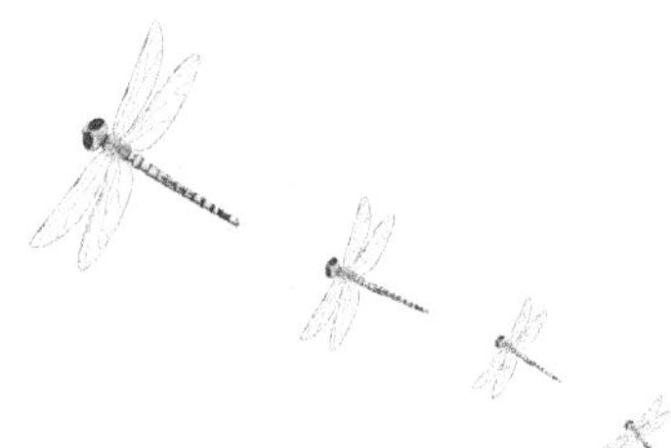

Final Summary of
Dragonfly Where Faith Takes Flight
A Christian Journey of Transformation"

"Dragonfly Where Faith Takes Flight" offers a Christian perspective on the transformative journey of faith, paralleling the metamorphosis of a dragonfly with the spiritual renewal promised in Christ. This book outlines a ten-step path designed to guide you through deep personal and spiritual change, drawing heavily on biblical principles and the life of Jesus as models for living a transformed life.

1. **Understanding Your Current State**: The journey begins with self-assessment, recognizing and accepting where you are spiritually and emotionally, with encouragement to invite God into the process of personal reflection.

2. **Embracing Change**: You are taught to see change not as a threat but as an opportunity for growth, underpinned by trust in God's plan and His word.

3. **Setting Concrete Goals**: This step focuses on aligning personal goals with God's will, using biblical guidance to set and pursue objectives that foster spiritual growth and meaningful living.

4. **Cultivating Resilience**: Building resilience through faith involves relying on God's strength in times of difficulty and embracing trials as opportunities for growth, modeled by biblical figures who demonstrated steadfast faith.

5. **Practicing Forgiveness**: Forgiveness is presented as essential for spiritual freedom and healing, requiring believers to extend grace as freely as it has been received from Christ.

6. **Overcoming Trauma**: The book addresses healing from trauma through the lens of faith, emphasizing God's nearness in suffering and the healing power of the Holy Spirit.

7. **Managing Loss and Grief**: Learning to cope with loss through biblical wisdom on mourning and the Christian hope in eternal life, emphasizing the supportive role of the Christian community.

8. **Reinventing Yourself**: This step involves a conscious decision to align your life more closely with Christian values, aiming for a holistic change that affects all areas of personal and professional life.

9. **Maintaining Your New Self**: Sustaining change is discussed in terms of ongoing spiritual practices, continuous learning, and active community engagement to prevent backsliding and promote lasting growth.

10. **Living as a Dragonfly**: The final step calls for living out the transformation daily, actively applying the changes to all aspects of life, and continuously growing in faith and service to God.

Each chapter of "Dragonfly Where Faith Takes Flight" is designed not only to guide you through personal transformation but also to deepen your relationship with God. It encourages a reflective and active approach to faith that involves regular prayer, study of Scripture, and community involvement. The book concludes by reinforcing the idea that Christian transformation is a lifelong journey of becoming more like Christ, advocating for a dynamic faith that influences every action and interaction.

In summary, "Dragonfly Where Faith Takes Flight" serves as both a roadmap and companion for you to fundamentally transform your life through Christ, embodying the resilience, renewal, and beauty of a dragonfly in your spiritual journey.

Notes